DIABET

DIABETIC
Desserts

Healthy puddings for those with a sweet tooth

Sue Hall

THORSONS PUBLISHING GROUP

First published in 1989

© SUE HALL 1989

British Library Cataloguing in Publication Data

Hall, Sue, *1962-*
Diabetics desserts.
1. Diabetics. Food: Sweet dishes — Recipes
I. Title
641.8'6

ISBN 0-7225-1653-3

Colour photography and styling by
Stonecastle Graphics, Maidstone, Kent
Illustrations by Andre Yaniw

*Published by Thorsons Publishers Limited, Wellingborough,
Northamptonshire, NN8 2RQ, England*

Typeset by Harper Phototypesetters Limited, Northampton
Printed in Great Britain by Richard Clay Limited,
Bungay, Suffolk

1 3 5 7 9 10 8 6 4 2

Acknowledgements

The author would like to thank Andy for support and tasting, Sally for typing and Janet for inspiring the book.

Contents

Recipes

Throughout the book I have used this standard conversion chart:

Weights

25g	— 1 oz
50g	— 2 oz
75g	— 3 oz
100g	— 4 oz
150g	— 5 oz
175g	— 6 oz
200g	— 7 oz
225g	— 8 oz
250g	— 9 oz
275g	— 10 oz
300g	— 11 oz
350g	— 12 oz
375g	— 13 oz
400g	— 14 oz
425g	— 15 oz
450g	— 16 oz

Liquid Measures

150ml — ¼ pint
275ml — ½ pint
425ml — ¾ pint
550ml — 1 pint

Spoon Measures

1 teaspoon — 5ml
1 dessertspoon — 10ml
1 tablespoon — 15ml

It is best to use this to get accurate results.

Comparative Oven Temperatures are given below:

Oven Temperatures

Fahrenheit	Centigrade	Gas
300°	150°	No. 2
325°	160°	No. 3
350°	180°	No. 4
375°	190°	No. 5
400°	200°	No. 6
425°	220°	No. 7
450°	230°	No. 8

Introduction

Being a diabetic and eating a healthy diet does not necessarily mean giving up desserts and puddings, but it does mean you'll have to take care to include only those which are suitable and which fit into your total food plan.

Diabetics who have a carbohydrate and calories allowance really should try to stick to it — if you are having problems understanding your food plan or keeping to it, go back to your doctor or dietitian for more help and practical advice. If you are following a reducing diet or need to lose weight be sure to choose desserts carefully to fit into your daily calories. The aim of this book, then, is to provide a wide range of high-fibre, reduced-fat, low-sugar recipes for everyday eating or entertaining.

To obtain good control of diabetes, it is important to eat regularly and in the correct quantities. Diet is an important part of good balance. A simple way of guiding your food choices is to use the traffic light system. This will help all of you — even those with no carbohydrate or calorie allowance — to select suitable foods. This traffic light system is used in the BDA book *Countdown* (see the Recommended Reading list on page 99).

Think of your diet instructions as a set of traffic lights directing your diet:

GREEN for foods you should use; i.e., high-fibre, low-fat, low-sugar.
AMBER for foods you can use with caution; i.e., medium-fibre, medium-fat, medium-sugar.
RED for foods which should not be used regularly but may be used on special occasions; i.e., high-fat, low-fibre or high-sugar.

RED — STOP
Don't use these foods except on
special occasions.

AMBER — CAUTION
Use these foods with care and
not as the largest part of the diet.

GREEN — GO
Use these foods regularly.

Why Do We Stress High-fibre?
A high-fibre intake is widely publicized as being important to the
diabetic diet — helping to stabilize blood sugar levels, preventing
low or high sugars, and generally improving control. Most people
following a high-fibre diet find their control improves generally and
they experience fewer 'hypos' — it is also good general policy for
all of us to eat lots of fibre of course. So the recipes in this book
will help to improve your carbohydrate choices.

What About Fat?
A fairly low total fat intake is part of a good eating plan for all of
us because now it is generally accepted that most people benefit
from eating less fat and using vegetable rather than animal fats.
The following recipes will help you to lower your total fat intake.

About the Recipes
The recipes show the total carbohydrate and calorie content and
a suggestion for the number of portions, with a freezing note to
help your planning. All the recipes have been thoroughly tested.
All spoon measures are level and you should only use the Imperial

or the Metric measurements — not mix the two (the recipes have been calculated using the Metric measurements).

Important Ingredients
A few notes about products you may not have used before.

Flour
All of these flours are made by several companies and are available in health food shops and many supermarkets.

(a) *Wholemeal and Wholemeal Self-raising.* These are 100 per cent wholemeal flours — containing lots of fibre (you will see I've used them in bread, cakes, puddings and sauces). The self-raising version should always be used if it is specified in a recipe.

(b) *81 per cent Plain and Self-raising.* The figure 81 per cent refers to the extraction rates of the flour during milling, i.e., the amount of the grain left in the flour. These, therefore, contain less fibre than wholemeal but more than white flour. These are still a good compromise choice and often produce lighter results than wholemeal. If a recipe specifies 81 per cent flour then this should be used to obtain a good result and keep the carbohydrate and calorie figures right.

Low-fat Spread/Margarine
Always use the fat I have specified — again any change will affect the calories and the finished product. If you are using a low-fat spread choose one of vegetable origin. These are widely available in most supermarkets. Choose soft margarine, not hard.

Fructose (Fruit Sugar)
This is a bulk sweetener sold under the brand names of 'Dietade' or 'Fruisana' in chemists and supermarkets. In these recipes I have followed normal BDA policy of not counting the carbohydrate so long as one does not have more than 1 oz (25g) per day. If you

use lots of sweet recipes in one day or eat fructose or sorbitol in other things, you will need to bear in mind the amount of fructose you are eating. The calories in fructose are always counted.

1. Are Diabetic Desserts a Good Idea?

I am sure some of you are wondering why a whole book should be devoted to a part of our eating habits many diabetics feel must be restricted. When diagnosed, diabetics are told to avoid large quantities of sugar and to cut down on sweet products. Surely to follow a 'healthy' diet one should cut out pudding. This of course is not strictly true. More and more diabetics are being encouraged to lead a 'normal' life and eat 'normal' food like everyone else. Most of us can quite easily cut down on our fat and increase our fibre in savoury dishes, but cakes and puddings are rather more difficult. This book is designed to help you adapt your favourite pudding recipes and try lots of new ideas — ideas which have been especially created to fit into the diabetic food plan of high-fibre, reduced-fat and reduced-sugar.

That is not to say, of course, that you can eat huge helpings of these puddings without any regard to your diabetes. They must be fitted into your carbohydrate and calorie intakes and should form part of a healthy eating plan. Some of them are designed for special occasions and should be thought of as treats. A pudding which is part of a high-fibre, low-fat, low-sugar meal can play a part in any healthy diet. It can also help the whole family to eat a more healthy diet without feeling they are missing out. Of course you will all use the book in different ways — some families eat a pudding every day, whilst others save them for Sunday lunch or occasional treats.

If you are on a reducing diet or your dietitian is encouraging you to lose weight, you must be especially careful to choose puddings which fit into your allowance and to cut your portion *carefully*! If you don't get the number of portions I have suggested from a dish you are being too generous!

You will notice I have avoided the use of artificial sweeteners wherever possible; there are two reasons for this:

1. Many people are keen to cut down the amount of artifical substances of any type in their food.

2. It is a good idea to try to educate yourself to have a less sweet tooth.

However if you find some of the dishes too tart, use a non-calorie sweetener (usually liquid or tablet) to sweeten them to taste. Your dietitian can suggest an actual brand.

Once you've tried some of these desserts you may want to have a go at adapting your own *or* creating new ones. There are several basic guidelines which may help.

1. Try to replace any white flour with 81 per cent or wholemeal varieties.

2. Take out sugar — replace it with either:

   (a) half the quantity of fructose
   (b) dried fruit
   (c) a non-calorie artificial sweetener.

Only use the first alternative if the sugar plays a role in the structure of the dish i.e., it forms the bulk e.g., in a creamed sponge. If the sugar is only used to sweeten fruit or a crumble mixture use alternatives (b) or (c).

3. Use a polyunsaturated margarine instead of butter, hard margarine or lard.

4. Use skimmed or semi-skimmed milk instead of whole.

5. Use fromage frais, natural yogurt or whipping cream in place of double cream.

6. Use quark, fromage frais or cottage cheese in place of full fat cream cheese.

7.   If you are using dried fruit in a recipe then soak it in the liquid from the dish for 2–3 hours to draw the sweetness out of the fruit (see Stuffed Oranges, page 60).

8.   Always buy fruit tinned in natural juice *not* syrup, and watch out for low-fat versions of evaporated milk, etc.

If you do not have the time to make a pudding, do not revert to a high-sugar commercial product — eat a piece of fresh fruit *or* use your *Countdown* book (see Recommended Reading list, page 99) to choose a slightly healthier bought pudding. For instance, rice pudding or instant pudding are now available in low-sugar versions.

Enjoy your desserts and have fun trying out all the new ideas!

2. Winter Desserts

Minty Fruit

Serves 4   Total CHO — 100g   Total Cals — 350

8 dried apricots,
  chopped
2 fresh peaches,
  chopped
2 medium bananas,
  sliced
2 red apples, sliced
2 teaspoons lemon
  juice
2 tablespoons dry
  cider
2 teaspoons clear
  honey
12 fresh mint leaves,
  chopped

1. Mix fruits and place in a flame-proof dish, add remaining ingredients and stir.
2. Cover and bake at 180°C/350°F (Gas Mark 4) for 20 minutes.
3. Serve hot or chilled.

Each portion contains 25g CHO and 90 calories.

Note: This recipe is *not* suitable for freezing.

Orange and Apple Brown Betty

Serves 2   Total CHO — 60g   Total Cals — 640

2 eating apples,
peeled and chopped
Juice and rind of 1
large orange
2 oz (50g) wholemeal
self-raising flour
2 oz (50g)
polyunsaturated
margarine
½ teaspoon ground
nutmeg

1. Place the fruit, juice and rind in the base of a small casserole dish.
2. Mix the remaining ingredients well and sprinkle over the fruit.
3. Bake at 180°C/350°F (Gas Mark 4) for 30 minutes. Serve hot or cold.

Each portion contains 30g CHO and 320 calories.

Note: This recipe freezes well.

Apricot and Almond Pudding

Serves 4   Total CHO — 85g   Total Cals — 830

14 oz (400g) tin
apricots in natural
juice
2 oz (50g) ground
almonds
4 oz (100g) wholemeal
bread (about 4 slices)
Enough skimmed
milk to bring apricot
juice to ½ pint
(275ml)
2 size 3 eggs, beaten
Nutmeg, to taste

1. Drain the apricots, reserving the juice. Place alternate layers of fruit, almonds and torn up bread in a deep oven-proof dish.
2. Mix the reserved juice with enough milk to give ½ pint (275ml). Add the eggs and nutmeg, and beat together.
3. Pour the milk mixture over the fruit and nut base.
4. Bake at 180°C/350°F (Gas Mark 4) for 1 hour. Serve immediately.

Each portion contains 20g CHO and 210 calories.

Note: This recipe is *not* suitable for freezing.

Apricot Upside-down Pudding

Serves 5   Total CHO — 140g   Total Cals — 1655

*14 oz (400g) tin
apricots in natural
juice
2 size 3 eggs
5 oz (150g) wholemeal
self-raising flour
3 oz (75g)
polyunsaturated
margarine
2 oz (50g) fructose
(fruit sugar)*

1. Drain the apricots (reserving the juice) and place in the base of a lightly-oiled ovenproof dish. Pour on 4 tablespoons of natural juice.
2. Beat all the remaining ingredients together well with enough juice to give a soft dropping consistency.
3. Spoon the sponge mix over the fruit and bake at 350°F/180°C (Gas Mark 4) for 40–50 minutes. Turn out carefully and serve warm.

Each portion contains 30g CHO and 330 calories.

Note: This recipe freezes well.

Plums in a Veil

Serves 5   Total CHO — 100g   Total Cals — 1300

2lb (900g) ripe red plums
8 tablespoons fresh wholemeal breadcrumbs
2 oz (50g) polyunsaturated margarine
¼ pint (150ml) whipping cream
1 size 3 egg white

1. Stone the plums and poach them in a little water until tender. Drain well and allow to cool.
2. Toast the breadcrumbs and place in layers with the plums in a serving dish.
3. Whip the cream to soft peaks and whisk the egg white until stiff. Fold together. Spread over the plums.
4. Chill before serving.

Each portion contains 20g CHO and 260 calories.

Note: This recipe is not suitable for freezing.

Peach and Apple Nutty Crumble

Serves 4   Total CHO — 135g   Total Cals — 1820

14 oz (400g) tin peaches in natural juice
1 medium cooking apple, peeled, cored and sliced
2 oz (50g) desiccated coconut
2 oz (50g) mixed nuts, chopped
3 oz (75g) wholemeal flour
4 oz (100g) polyunsaturated margarine
1 oz (25g) rolled oats

1. Place the fruits and fruit juice in the base of an ovenproof dish.
2. Mix the remaining ingredients together to a crumble consistency and spoon over the fruit.
3. Bake at 350°F/180°C (Gas Mark 4) for 30 minutes. Serve hot.

Each portion contains about 30g CHO and 455 calories.

Note: This recipe freezes well *raw*.

Plum Sponge Layer

Serves 5   Total CHO — 180g   Total Cals — 1580

*1 lb (450g) plums,
stoned
6 oz (175g) 81 per
cent self-raising flour
2 size 3 eggs
1 oz (25g) fructose
(fruit sugar)
3 oz (75g)
polyunsaturated
margarine
3 tablespoons semi-
skimmed milk*

1. Stew the plums gently in their own juice until just tender. Place in the base of an ovenproof dish.
2. Beat all the remaining ingredients together (a food processor works well here).
3. Spoon the sponge mixture over the fruit and bake at 350°F/180°C (Gas Mark 4) for 30–40 minutes until risen and golden. Serve hot.

Each portion contains 35g CHO and 315 calories.

Note: This recipe is *not* suitable for freezing.

Sultana and Gooseberry Pudding

Serves 5   Total CHO — 190g   Total Cals — 1620

*2 oz (50g) sultanas
1 lb (450g)
gooseberries, topped
and tailed
6 oz (175g) 81 per
cent self-raising flour
2 size 3 eggs
1 oz (25g) fructose
(fruit sugar)
3 oz (75g)
polyunsaturated
margarine
3 tablespoons semi-
skimmed milk*

1. Stew the sultanas and gooseberries in their own juice until just tender. Place in the base of an oven-proof dish.
2. Beat all the remaining ingredients together (a food processor works well here).
3. Spoon the sponge mixture over the fruit and bake at 350°F/180°C (Gas Mark 4) for 30–40 minutes until risen and golden. Serve hot.

Each portion contains about 40g CHO and 325 calories.

Note: This recipe is *not* suitable for freezing.

Banana Sponge Pudding

Serves 5   Total CHO — 170g   Total Cals — 1500

2 medium bananas, mashed
6 oz (175g) 81 per cent self-raising flour
2 size 3 eggs
1 oz (25g) fructose (fruit sugar)
3 oz (75g) polyunsaturated margarine
2 tablespoons skimmed milk

1. Beat all the ingredients together well until a soft dropping consistency is achieved.
2. Pour into an oven-proof dish and bake at 350°F/180°C (Gas Mark 4) for 30–40 minutes until risen and golden. Serve hot.

Each portion contains 35g CHO and 300 calories.

Note: This recipe is not suitable for freezing.

Spice and Sultana Steamed Pud

Serves 6   Total CHO — 175g   Total Cals — 1610

3 oz (75g)
polyunsaturated
margarine
1 oz (25g) fructose
(fruit sugar)
3 size 3 eggs
6 oz (175g) 81 per
cent self-raising flour
2 oz (50g) sultanas
1 teaspoon mixed
spice

1. Cream the margarine and fructose until light and fluffy. Beat in remaining ingredients.
2. Place in a 1½ pint (825ml) basin, cover with foil and steam for 1¼ hours.
3. Turn out and serve.

Each portion contains 30g CHO and 270 calories.

Note: This recipe is *not* suitable for freezing.

Steaming Hints:
(a) Add 1 tablespoon of vinegar to your water to avoid staining your pan.
(b) Remember to top up the water if necessary during cooking.
(c) When covering your pudding, make a pleat in your foil or greaseproof paper to allow the pudding to rise.
(d) Put a strip of paper, foil or cloth under your bowl to make the pudding easier to lift out when hot.

Caribbean Flan

Serves 8   Total CHO — 200g   Total Cals — 1655

Pastry
*3 oz (75g)
polyunsaturated
margarine*
*6 oz (175g) 81 per
cent self-raising flour*
*Cold water, as
necessary*

Filling
*14 oz (400g) tin of
pineapple in natural
juice, drained and
chopped*
*5 oz (150g) cottage
cheese*
*2 size 3 eggs,
separated*
*2 teaspoons rum
(optional)*

1. Make the pastry by rubbing the fat into the flour and bringing to a soft dough with a little cold water. Chill for 15 minutes.
2. Roll out and line an 8-inch (20cm) flan ring.
3. Mix the pineapple, cheese, egg yolks and rum. Whisk the egg whites to stiff peaks.
4. Gently fold the egg whites into the cheese mixture. Pour into the pastry case.
5. Bake at 200°C/400°F (Gas Mark 6) for 20 minutes. Allow to cool in the flan ring.

Each portion contains 25g CHO and 205 calories.

Note: This recipe is *not* suitable for freezing *but* the raw pastry freezes well.

Pear and Mincemeat Flan

Serves 5   Total CHO — 200g   Total Cals — 1480

Pastry
*3 oz (75g)
polyunsaturated
margarine
6 oz (175g) wholemeal
flour
Cold water, as
necessary*

Filling
*4 oz (100g) reduced-
sugar mincemeat,
bought or see page 67
5 pears, freshly peeled,
cored and sliced*

1. Make the pastry by rubbing the fat into the flour and bring to a soft dough with a little cold water. (The food processor makes good pastry.)

2. Roll out and line a 7-inch (18cm) flan ring. Chill for 10 minutes.

3. Spread the mincemeat over the base and top with the sliced pears.

4. Bake at 375°F/190°C (Gas Mark 5) for 25 minutes. Serve hot or cold.

Each portion contains 40g CHO and 300 calories.

Note: This recipe freezes well.

Pear and Almond Flan

Serves 6   Total CHO — 180g   Total Cals — 2370

Pastry
2 oz (50g)
polyunsaturated
margarine
6 oz (175g) 81 per
cent plain flour
Cold water, as
necessary

Filling
3oz (75g)
polyunsaturated
margarine
1 tablespoon clear
honey
2 size 3 eggs
4 oz (100g) ground
almonds
14 oz (400g) tin
pears, drained or 3
fresh pears, halved
and poached

1. Make the pastry by rubbing the fat into the flour and bringing to a soft dough with a little cold water.

2. Roll out and line an 8-inch (20cm) flan dish. Bake blind at 200°C/400°F (Gas Mark 6) for 15 minutes. Allow to cool.

3. Mix all of the filling ingredients together, except the pears. Pour into the base.

4. Arrange the pear halves on top of the filling. Bake at 190°C/375°F (Gas Mark 5) for 30–40 minutes until risen and firm to the touch. Serve hot or cold.

Each portion contains 30g CHO and 395 calories.

Note: This recipe freezes well.

Fruity Custard Flan

Serves 8   Total CHO — 265g   Total Cals — 1820

Pastry
2 oz (50g)
polyunsatured
margarine
6 oz (175g) 81 per
cent plain flour
Cold water, as
necessary

Filling
8 oz (225g) dried fruit
salad, soaked, drained
and chopped
2 size 3 eggs
½ pint (275ml)
skimmed evaporated
milk

1. Make the pastry by rubbing the fat into the flour and bringing to a soft dough with a little cold water.
2. Roll out and line an 8-inch (20cm) flan dish. Bake blind at 200°C/400°F (Gas Mark 6) for 15 minutes. Allow to cool.
3. Place the fruit salad in the bottom of the flan case.
4. Mix the eggs and milk, pour over the fruit and bake at 180°C/350°F (Gas Mark 4)) for 30–40 minutes until set. Serve hot or cold.

Each portion contains 35g CHO and 230 calories.

Note: This recipe is *not* suitable for freezing, but the pastry freezes well raw.

Chocolate Rice Pudding

Serves 3   Total CHO — 65g   Total Cals — 425

2 oz (50g) brown
pudding rice
¾ pint (425ml) semi-
skimmed milk
½ oz (15g) carob
powder

1. Stir all the ingredients together well —
ensuring the carob is well mixed in.
2. Pour into an oven-proof dish and bake
at 300°F/150°C (Gas Mark 2) for 1 hour.
Serve hot or cold.

Each portion contains 20g CHO and 140
calories.

Note: This recipe is *not* suitable for
freezing.

Fruity Rice Pudding

Serves 2   Total CHO — 80g   Total Cals — 440

2 oz (50g) brown
pudding rice
½ pint (275ml) semi-
skimmed milk
1 oz (25g) raisins
1 oz (25g) glacé
cherries, chopped

1. Stir all the ingredients together well.
2. Pour into an oven-proof dish and bake
at 300°F/150°C (Gas Mark 2) for 1 hour.
Serve hot or cold.

Each portion contains 40g CHO and 220
calories.

Note: This recipe is *not* suitable for
freezing.

Wholemeal Crêpes

Makes 8   Total CHO — 80g   Total Cals — 485

4 oz (100g)
wholemeal flour
Pinch of salt
1 size 3 egg, beaten
½ pint (275ml)
skimmed milk
Oil, for frying

1. Beat all the ingredients, except the oil, together well until a smooth batter is formed. Leave to stand for 30 minutes.
2. Heat a little oil in a heavy-based pan and cook 8 crêpes — stack the cooked crêpes separated by layers of greaseproof paper.
3. Fill as desired but remember to add the filling figures to pancake figures. For filling suggestions see following pages.

Each pancake contains 10g CHO and 60 calories.

Note: These pancakes freeze well empty, separated by layers of greaseproof paper.

Boozy Orange Crêpes

Makes 8   Total CHO — 110g   Total Cals — 600

3 large oranges,
peeled and segments
skinned
2 tablespoons
Cointreau
8 wholemeal crêpes
(see above)

1. Chop the oranges and leave to soak in the Cointreau for 1 hour.
2. Use to fill the crêpes. Serve chilled.

Each crêpe (i.e., crêpe plus ⅛ filling) contains about 15g CHO and 75 calories.

Note: This recipe is *not* suitable for freezing.

Apple and Cinnamon Pancake Layer

Serves 8   Total CHO — 110g   Total Cals — 600

12 oz (350g) cooking
apples, peeled and
cored
2 teaspoons
cinnamon
8 wholemeal crêpes
(see page 31)

1. Chop the apples, add the cinnamon and stew in 2 teaspoons of water until soft — mash and allow to cool.

2. Use the apple mixture to sandwich the crêpes in a stack. Slice into 8 before serving.

Each portion contains about 15g CHO and 75 calories.

Note: This recipe is *not* suitable for freezing.

Banana Crêpes

Serves 8   Total CHO — 140g   Total Cals — 725

4 medium bananas,
mashed
5 oz (150g) carton of
set low-fat natural
yogurt
8 wholemeal crêpes
(see page 31)

1. Mix the bananas and yogurt together well.

2. Use to fill the crêpes. Chill for 15 minutes and serve.

Each crêpe (i.e., 1 crêpe plus ⅛ filling) contains about 20g CHO and 90 calories.

Note: This recipe is *not* suitable for freezing.

Boozy Oats

Serves 4	Total CHO — 40g	Total Cals — 1125

2 oz (50g) coarse
oatmeal
2 tablespoons whisky
1 tablespoon clear
honey
½ pint (275ml)
whipping cream

1. Soak the oatmeal in the whisky and honey for 15 minutes.
2. Cook over a gentle heat for 2 minutes, stirring all the time. Allow to cool.
3. Whip the cream. Gently fold into the oat mixture.
4. Chill for 2 hours.

Each portion contains 10g CHO and 280 calories.

Note: This recipe is *not* suitable for freezing.

Ginger Steamed Pud

Serves 5   Total CHO — 140g   Total Cals — 1480

3 oz (75g)
polyunsaturated
margarine
1 oz (25g) fructose
(fruit sugar)
3 size 3 eggs
6 oz (175g) 81 per
cent self-raising flour
2 teaspoons ground
ginger

1. Cream the margarine and fructose until light and fluffy. Beat in the remaining ingredients.
2. Place in a 1½ pint (825ml) basin, cover with foil and steam for 1¼ hours.
3. Turn out and serve.

Each portion contains almost 30g CHO and 300 calories.

Note: This recipe is not suitable for freezing. Steaming hints can be found on page 27.

Shortcrust Pastry

Makes 8 oz (225g) quantity   Total CHO — 150g
Total Cals — 1445

8 oz (225g)
wholemeal flour
4 oz (100g)
polyunsaturated
margarine
Cold water, as
necessary

1. Place the flour in a large bowl, rub in the fat until the mixture resembles fine breadcrumbs.
2. Bring to a soft dough with a little cold water. Use as required.

Note: This pastry freezes well *raw*.

Apple and Raisin Tart

Serves 6   Total CHO — 220   Total Cals — 1700

8 oz (225g) shortcrust
pastry (see above)
1 lb (450g) cooking
apples, peeled, cored
and sliced
2 oz (50g) raisins

1. Roll half the pastry and line a 9-inch (23cm) pie plate.
2. Place the apples and raisins on the pastry and top with the remaining pastry. Seal the edges.
3. Bake at 375°F/190°C (Gas Mark 5) for 30 minutes. Serve hot or cold.

Each portion contains 35g CHO and 280 calories.

Note: This recipe freezes well *raw*.

Plum and Almond Pie

Serves 6   Total CHO — 190g   Total Cals — 1890

---

8 oz (225g) shortcrust
pastry (see page 35)
1 lb (450g) plums,
stoned and chopped
2 oz (50g) almonds,
chopped

1. Roll half the pastry to line a 9-inch (23cm) pie plate.
2. Place the plums and nuts on the pastry and top with the remaining pastry. Seal the edges.
3. Bake at 375°F/190°C (Gas Mark 5) for 30 minutes. Serve hot or cold.

Each portion contains 30g CHO and 315 calories.

Note: This recipe freezes well *raw*.

3. Summer Desserts

Creamy Orange Whip

Serves 4	Total CHO — 10g	Total Cals — 115

¾ *pint (425ml)* made up *low-calorie orange squash**
1 *sachet gelatine*
2 *tablespoons boiling water*
5 *oz (150g) carton low-fat natural yogurt*

1. Place the squash in a measuring jug.
2. Dissolve the gelatine in the water and stir into the squash.
3. Leave until almost set.
4. Pour into a large bowl and quickly whisk in the yogurt until frothy.
5. Leave to set.

Each portion contains neg CHO and 30 calories.

Note: This recipe is *not* suitable for freezing.

*Use squashes made without artificial colours or flavourings wherever possible.

Green Apple Jelly

Serves 5   Total CHO — 70g   Total Cals — 260

*1 pint (550ml)
unsweetened apple
juice
1 sachet gelatine
2 tablespoons boiling
water
Natural green
colouring (optional)*

1. Place the juice in a serving dish.
2. Dissolve the gelatine in the water. Stir into the juice.
3. Colour if desired. Leave to set.

Each portion contains almost 15g CHO and 50 calories.

Note: This recipe is *not* suitable for freezing.

Blackcurrant Whip

Serves 4   Total CHO — 20g   Total Cals — 300

*¾ pint (425ml) made
up low-calorie
blackcurrant squash*
1 sachet gelatine
2 tablespoons boiling
water
5 oz (150g) tin
unsweetened
evaporated milk*

1. Place the squash in a measuring jug.
2. Dissolve the gelatine in the water and stir into the squash.
3. Leave until almost set.
4. Pour into a large bowl and whisk in the milk until frothy. Leave to set.

Each portion contains 5g CHO and 75 calories.

Note: This recipe is *not* suitable for freezing.

*Use squashes made without artificial colours or flavourings wherever possible.

Apple Snow

Serves 2   Total CHO — 20g   Total Cals — 100

2 large eating apples, cored and grated
Lemon juice
2 size 3 egg whites

1. Toss the apple in a little lemon juice.
2. Whisk the egg whites to stiff peaks, fold in the apple mixture and serve.

Each portion contains 10g CHO and 50 calories.

Note: This recipe is *not* suitable for freezing.

Real Blancmange

Serves 6   Total CHO — 60g   Total Cals — 320

2 tablespoons cornflour
1 pint (550ml) skimmed milk
Rind of 1 lemon
Juice of 2 oranges

1. Mix the cornflour and a little milk to a smooth paste
2. Heat remaining milk to boiling point, pour onto the paste, return to the pan and bring to the boil, stirring continuously and cook for 2 minutes. Allow to cool.
3. Stir in the rind and juice, pour into a mould and chill for 2 hours.

Each portion contains 10g CHO and 55 calories.

Note: This recipe is *not* suitable for freezing and should be used on the day it is made.

Jelly Castles

Makes 5   Total CHO — 40g   Total Cals — 340

---

*1 carton (200ml)
semi-skimmed
unsweetened
evaporated milk
¼ pint (150ml)
unsweetened orange
juice
1 sachet gelatine
2 tablespoons boiling
water*

1. Mix the milk and juice together well.
2. Dissolve the gelatine in the water and beat into the milk and juice.
3. Pour into 5 dariole moulds and place in the refrigerator until set.
4. Turn out and serve.

Each castle contains almost 10g CHO and 70 calories.

Note: This recipe is *not* suitable for freezing.

Two-colour Fruit Salad

'A designer pudding'

Serves 4   Total CHO — 80g   Total Cals — 325

---

*½ medium melon
4 oz (100g) fresh
green figs, sliced
lengthways
4 oz (100g) green
grapes, halved
2 kiwi fruit, sliced
1 small pear
¼ pint (150ml)
unsweetened white
grape juice*

1. Scoop the melon flesh into balls and mix with the rest of the fruit.
2. Pour on the juice and chill for 2 hours.

Each portion contains 20g CHO and 80 calories.

Note: This recipe is *not* suitable for freezing.

Spicy Fruit Salad

Serves 5   Total CHO — 75g   Total Cals — 260

1 green chilli
½ pint (275ml) water
2 bananas, sliced
2 red apples, cored
and sliced
8 oz (225g) fresh
apricots, stoned
1 pear, cored and
chopped

1. Deseed the chilli and chop finely
2. Heat the water and chilli to boiling point and leave to cool. Sieve out the chilli.
3. Mix all the fruits together and pour on the water. Chill and serve.

Each portion contains 15g CHO and 50 calories.

Note: This recipe is *not* suitable for freezing.

Hot Fruit Salad

Serves 5   Total CHO — 80g   Total Cals — 280

¼ pint (150ml) dry
red wine
1 cinnamon stick
2 green apples, cored
and chopped
2 bananas, sliced
3 oz (75g) black
grapes
2 pears, cored and
sliced

1. Heat the wine and cinnamon stick to boiling point — reduce the heat and simmer for 3 minutes.
2. Stir the fruit into the wine, heat for 2 minutes and serve.

Each portion contains 15g CHO and 55 calories.

Note: This recipe is *not* suitable for freezing.

Pears in Red Wine

Serves 2   Total CHO — 20g   Total Cals — 80

2 pears, peeled and
cored
¼ pint (150ml) dry
red wine

1. Place the pears in an oven-proof dish, pour on the wine.
2. Bake at 150°C/300°F (Gas Mark 2) until the pears are tender (about 30 minutes) turning the pears occasionally.
3. Allow to cool before serving.

Each portion contains 10g CHO and 40 calories.

Note: This recipe is not suitable for freezing.

Cheesy Peaches

Serves 2   Total CHO — 20g   Total Cals — 175

2 fresh peaches,
stoned and halved
4 oz (100g) cottage
cheese, well drained

1. Place the peach halves cut side up on a plate.
2. Fill the centres with cottage cheese. Chill and serve.

Each portion (i.e., 2 halves and cheese) contains 10g CHO and 90 calories.

Note: This recipe is not suitable for freezing.

Home-made Fruit Yogurt

Makes 1 pint (550ml)   Total CHO — 40g   Total Cals 330

1 pint (550ml) semi-
skimmed milk
2 tablespoons natural
yogurt
4 oz (100g) chopped
fresh fruit

1. Heat the milk to boiling point, simmer for 2 minutes and allow to cool to 43°C/110°F.
2. Stir in the yogurt, pour into a wide-neck flask and leave in a warm place for 8 hours.
3. Remove any excess liquid from the surface and stir in the fruit.
4. Store for up to 1 week in a refrigerator.

Note: This recipe is *not* suitable for freezing.

Nutty Rice

Serves 4   Total CHO — 110g   Total Cals — 1140

3 oz (75g) brown
pudding rice
2 oz (50g) desiccated
coconut
2 oz (50g) ground
almonds
1 oz (25g) chopped
dates
1 pint (550ml)
skimmed milk
A little ground
nutmeg

1. Mix all the ingredients together well and place in an oven-proof dish.
2. Bake for 30 minutes at 200°C/400°F (Gas Mark 6) and then for 40 minutes at 150°C/300°F (Gas Mark 2). Serve immediately.

Each portion contains almost 30g CHO and 285 calories.

Note: This recipe is *not* suitable for freezing.

Rhubarb and Ricotta Dessert

Serves 4   Total CHO — 25g   Total Cals — 320

1 sachet gelatine
2 tablespoons boiling water
6 tablespoons unsweetened orange juice
4 oz (100g) rhubarb, stewed and drained
5 oz (150g) carton low-fat natural yogurt
4 oz (100g) Ricotta cheese
Juice of ½ lemon

1. Dissolve the gelatine in the water.
2. Process or blend all the ingredients together well. Allow to set.

Each portion contains about 5g CHO and 80 calories.

Note: This recipe is not suitable for freezing.

Crunchy Banana

Serves 2   Total CHO — 60   Total Cals — 395

2 × 5 oz (150g) cartons low-fat, no-sugar banana yogurt
1 oz (25g) bran flake breakfast cereal
1 small banana, sliced
1 oz (25g) chopped hazelnuts

1. Stir all the ingredients together well. Chill and serve.

Each portion contains 30g CHO and 200 calories.

Note: This recipe is not suitable for freezing.

Strawberry Shortcake

Serves 8   Total CHO — 200g   Total Cals — 3135

---

8 oz (225g)
wholemeal flour
5 oz (150g)
polyunsaturated
margarine
1 oz (25g) caster
sugar*
2 size 3 egg yolks
4 drops vanilla
essence
1 lb (450g)
strawberries, fresh
or frozen
½ pint (275ml)
whipping cream

1. Beat together the flour, margarine, sugar, egg yolks and vanilla essence. (A food processor works well here.)

2. Once a smooth paste is reached, set aside in a cool place for 1 hour.

3. Roll out two 9-inch (23cm) rounds and bake at 350°F/180°C (Gas Mark 4) for 15–20 minutes. Allow one round to cool whole — cut the other into 8 sections and leave to cool.

4. Clean the strawberries and chop. Whip the cream to stiff peaks and mix in the fruit.

5. Spread the cream mixture onto the whole shortcake, top with the shortcake sections and serve immediately.

Each portion contains 25g CHO and 390 calories.

Note: This recipe is *not* suitable for freezing.

* Divided between 8 people this quantity of sugar becomes irrelevant.

Spicy Fruit Compote

Serves 2   Total CHO — 40g   Total Cals — 160

½ pint (275ml)
boiling water
4 oz (100g) dried
fruit salad
¼ inch (0.5cm)
cinnamon stick
Pinch of chilli powder

1. Pour the boiling water over the other ingredients, which have been placed in a bowl.
2. Leave to stand for 8 hours.
or
Cover with cling-film, pierce the top and microwave on HIGH for 4 minutes, stir, and microwave for another 4 minutes. Allow to stand for 30 minutes.
3. Chill before serving.

Each portion contains 20g CHO and 80 calories.

Note: This recipe is *not* suitable for freezing.

Carob Base Cheesecake

Serves 6   Total CHO — 70g   Total Cals — 625

Base
½ oz (15g) minced
dried dates
2 fl oz (50ml) water
4 fl oz (100ml)
skimmed milk
1 oz (25g) carob
powder
2 Weetabix biscuits,
crumbled

Filling
1 size 3 egg,
separated
9 oz (250g) Quark
cheese
2 oz (50g) dried
apricots, chopped
1 tablespoon lemon
juice
2 fl oz (50ml) low-fat
natural yogurt

1. Cook the dates in the water, milk and carob powder until a thick smooth paste is formed. Stir in the Weetabix and press into the base of a 7-inch (18cm) cake tin.
2. Beat the egg yolk, cheese, apricots, lemon juice and yogurt together well. Fold in the whisked egg white.
3. Pour onto the base and bake at 180°C/350°F (Gas Mark 4) for 30 minutes. Allow to cool on a wire rack.

Each portion contains about 10g CHO and 105 calories.

Note: This recipe is *not* suitable for freezing.

Baked Cheesecake

| Serves 5 | Total CHO — 125 | Total Cals — 1860 |

Base
3 oz (75g)
polyunsaturated
margarine
4 oz (100g) oats
2 oz (50g) sultanas

Filling
2 oz (50g)
polyunsaturated
margarine
9 oz (250g) Quark
cheese
2 size 3 eggs
1 oz (25g) raisins
1 oz (25g) ground
almonds
Juice and rind of 1
lemon
2 tablespoons of low-
fat natural yogurt

1. Melt the base margarine, stir in the oats and sultanas.
2. Press into the base of a 7-inch (18cm) cake tin.
3. Bake at 180°C/350°F (Gas Mark 4) for 10 minutes. Allow to cool.
4. Beat all the filling ingredients together well, pour onto the base and bake at 180°C/350°F (Gas Mark 4) for 45 minutes. Serve hot or cold.

Each portion contains 25g CHO and 375 calories.

Note: This recipe is not suitable for freezing.

Chocolate Ice Box Cake

Serves 6   Total CHO — 100g   Total Cals — 1275

4 oz (100g) wholemeal sponge cake (stale cake is fine!)
1 pint (550ml) skimmed milk
2 oz (50g) fructose sweetened diabetic chocolate, melted
½ oz (15g) cornflour
5 oz (150g) carton whipping cream

1. Break the sponge into the base of the serving dish.
2. Heat the milk and chocolate gently until the chocolate has melted.
3. Beat in the cornflour, return to the heat and bring to the boil, stirring all the time.
4. Pour the chocolate mixture over the sponge. Allow to cool and then chill for 2 hours.
5. Top with whipped cream.

Each portion contains 15g CHO and 215 calories.

Note: This recipe is *not* suitable for freezing.

Banana Cheesecake

Serves 6   Total CHO — 160g   Total Cals — 1830

Base
*3 oz (75g)
polyunsaturated
margarine*
*6 oz (175g) digestives,
crushed*

Topping
*11 oz (300g) firm
tofu (soya bean curd)*
*4 oz (100g) cottage
cheese*
2 medium bananas
*Juice and rind of ½
lemon*

1. Melt the margarine, stir into the biscuits and press into the base of an 8-inch (20cm) loose-bottom flan ring. Leave to cool.

2. Beat all of the topping ingredients together well (a food processor works well here) and pour over the base.

3. Chill for 4 hours before serving.

Each portion contains 25g CHO and 305 calories.

Note: This recipe is *not* suitable for freezing.

Blackcherry Cheesecake

Serves 6   Total CHO — 175g   Total Cals — 1930

Base
3 oz (75g)
polyunsaturated
margarine
6 oz (175g) digestives,
crushed

Topping
11 oz (300g) firm tofu
(soya bean curd)
4 oz (100g) cottage
cheese
14 oz (400g) tin
blackcherries in
natural juice, drained
Juice and rind of ½
lemon

1. Melt the margarine, stir into the biscuits and press into the base of an 8-inch (20cm) loose-bottom flan ring. Leave to cool.

2. Beat all of the topping ingredients together well (a food processor works well here) and pour over the base.

3. Chill for 4 hours before serving.

Each portion contains 30g CHO and 320 calories.

Note: This recipe is not suitable for freezing.

Prune and Rum Mousse

Serves 4   Total CHO — 100g   Total Cals — 590

8 oz (225g) stoned
prunes, soaked
overnight
1 tablespoon dark
rum
2 size 3 eggs,
separated
5 oz (150ml) carton
low-fat natural yogurt

1. Stew the prunes in the minimum of water until soft (about 40 minutes). Drain well.

2. Purée the prunes, rum, egg yolks and yogurt together.

3. Whisk the egg whites to stiff peaks. Fold into the purée and chill before serving.

Each portion contains 25g CHO and 150 calories.

Note: This recipe is not suitable for freezing.

Apricot and Whisky Mousse

Serves 4   Total CHO — 100g   Total Cals — 635

8 oz (225g) dried
apricots, soaked
overnight
1 tablespoon whisky
2 size 3 eggs,
separated
5 oz (150g) carton
low-fat natural yogurt

1. Stew the apricots in the minimum of water until tender (about 40 minutes). Drain well.

2. Purée the apricots, whisky, egg yolks and yogurt together.

3. Whisk the egg whites to stiff peaks, fold into the purée and chill before serving.

Each portion contains 25g CHO and 160 calories.

Note: This recipe is not suitable for freezing.

4. Quick and Easy

Apricot Trifle

Serves 6   Total CHO — 85g   Total Cals — 975

14oz (400g) tin
apricots in natural
juice
1 sachet gelatine
2 tablespoons
boiling water
1 pint (550ml)
skimmed milk
2 dessertspoons
custard powder
5 oz (150g) carton
whipping cream

1. Drain the apricots (reserve the juice) and place in base of a serving dish.
2. Make the juice up to ¾ pint (425ml) with water.
3. Dissolve the gelatine in the water and stir into the juice. Pour onto the apricots and allow to set.
4. Make the custard, using the skimmed milk, allow to cool and pour over the jelly. Chill for 2 hours.
5. Whip the cream to stiff peaks and spoon over the custard.

Each portion contains 15g CHO and 165 calories.

Note: This recipe is *not* suitable for freezing.

Fluffy Fruit

Serves 2   Total CHO — 30g   Total Cals — 370

1 size 3 egg white
2 × 5 oz (150g)
cartons low-fat, no-
sugar fruit yogurt
2 oz (50g) chopped
mixed nuts

1. Whisk egg white to stiff peaks.
2. Fold into yogurt and nuts. Chill and serve.

Each portion contains 15g CHO and 125 calories.

Note: This recipe is *not* suitable for freezing.

Rum, Raisin and Apricot Yogurt

Serves 4   Total CHO — 120g   Total Cals — 610

12 oz (350g) low-fat
natural yogurt (page
43)
2 oz (50g) raisins
2 oz (50g)
wheatflakes breakfast
cereal
3 teaspoons rum
3 oz (75g) dried
apricots, chopped

1. Mix all of the ingredients together well, chill and serve.

Each portion contains 30g CHO and 150 calories.

Note: This recipe is *not* suitable for freezing.

Apricot Stuffed Apples

Serves 2   Total CHO — 70g   Total Cals — 290

---

2 medium cooking apples, washed and cored 2 oz (50g) dried apricots, chopped 1 oz (25g) raisins ¼ pint (150ml) water

1. Place the apples in an oven-proof dish. Slit the skins horizontally around the apple.

2. Stuff with the apricots and raisins. Pour the water into the base of the dish.

3. Bake at 350°F/180°C (Gas Mark 4) for 20–30 minutes until the apple is tender.

or

Microwave on MEDIUM for 10 minutes until the apples are tender.

4. Peel the skin from the top half of the apples and serve.

Each portion contains 35g CHO and 145 calories.

Note: This recipe is *not* suitable for freezing.

Poached Clementines

Serves 2   Total CHO — 20g   Total Cals — 80

*4 clementines,
washed
½ pint (275ml) cold
water*

1. Place the clementines and water in an oven-proof dish.
2. Bake at 350°F/180°C (Gas Mark 4) for 20–30 minutes.

or

Microwave on MEDIUM for 10 minutes.
3. Allow to cool in the water. Drain and serve.

Each portion (i.e., 2 clementines) contains 10g CHO and 40 calories.

Note: The whole clementines are eaten. These are delicious with home-made ice-cream *or* fromage frais.
This recipe is *not* suitable for freezing.

Muesli Cottage Cheese

Serves 1   Total CHO — 30g   Total Cals — 200

*3 oz (75g) cottage
cheese, drained
1 oz (25g)
unsweetened muesli
1 small banana,
sliced*

1. Mix all the ingredients together well. Chill and serve.

Note: This recipe is *not* suitable for freezing.

Perfect for a Summer wedding buffet: Apricot Trifle (page 53) and
Blackberry Mousse (page 92).

Two warming treats for a Winter Sunday lunch: Hot Fruit Salad (page 41) and Sultana and Gooseberry Pudding (page 23).

A selection of ingredients used in the Freeze Ahead chapter.

Ideal for long, hot Summer days: individual Creamy Orange Whips (page 37).

Delicious and low-calorie: Blackcurrant Whip (page 38) and Apple
Snow (page 39).

Strictly for special occasions!: Pineapple Cream (page 94) and
Chocolate Mousse (page 96).

Three puddings for when you're in a hurry: Two-colour Fruit Salad
(page 40), Rum, Raisin and Apricot Yogurt (page 54) and Cheesy
Peaches (page 42).

There is no need to feel left out at Christmas: Traditional Christmas Pudding (page 65).

Lime Pears

Serves 2   Total CHO — 20g   Total Cals — 80

2 medium eating pears, halved and cored
4 tablespoons low-calorie lime juice
1 cinnamon stick
¼ pint (150ml) water

1. Place all of the ingredients in an oven-proof dish.
2. Bake at 350°F/180°C (Gas Mark 4) for 30 minutes.

or

Microwave on MEDIUM for 10 minutes, turning pears over after 5 minutes.
3. Allow to cool in the juice — chill and serve.

Each portion (i.e., 2 halves) contains 10g CHO and 40 calories.

Note: This recipe is *not* suitable for freezing.

Apricots and Almonds
Serve with yogurt or fromage frais

Serves 3   Total CHO — 45g   Total Cals — 260

---

*1 lb (450g) fresh
apricots, stoned and
halved
1 oz (25g) chopped
almonds
¼ pint (150ml)
unsweetened apple
juice*

1. Place all of the ingredients in an oven-proof dish.
2. Bake at 350°F/180°C (Gas Mark 4) for 20–30 minutes.

or

Microwave on MEDIUM for 10 minutes.
3. Serve hot or cold.

Each portion contains 15g CHO and 85 calories.

Note: This recipe is *not* suitable for freezing.

Bananas 'Mac'
An unusual way to eat bananas

Serves 2   Total CHO — 45g   Total Cals — 280

---

2 medium firm
bananas, peeled and
split lengthways
1 oz (25g) glacé
cherries, chopped
1 oz (25g) desiccated
coconut
3 tablespoons green
ginger wine
¼ pint (150ml) water

1. Place the bananas in the base of an oven-proof dish.
2. Add the remaining ingredients.
3. Bake at 350°F/180°C (Gas Mark 4) for 20 minutes.

or

Microwave on MEDIUM for 6 minutes.
4. Serve hot or cold.

Each portion contains about 20g CHO and 140 calories.

Note: This recipe is *not* suitable for freezing.

Apple Cottage Cheese

Serves 1   Total CHO — 30g   Total Cals — 200

---

3 oz (75g) cottage
cheese, drained
1 oz (25g)
unsweetened muesli
1 small eating apple,
cored and chopped

1. Mix all the ingredients together well. Chill and serve.

Note: This recipe is *not* suitable for freezing.

Stuffed Oranges

Serves 2   Total CHO — 30g   Total Cals — 245

2 medium oranges
3 heaped tablespoons
    8 per cent fat
    fromage frais
2 tablespoons chopped
    mixed nuts
1 tablespoon raisins

1. Carefully slice the tops from the oranges and scoop out the flesh. Keep the skins whole.

2. Chop the flesh — removing the pips, etc.

3. Mix the flesh with the remaining ingredients and place inside the orange skins. Replace the tops.*

4. Chill for 2 hours and serve.

Each 'orange' contains 15g CHO and 120 calories.

Note: This recipe is *not* suitable for freezing.

* For a sweeter end result, mix the fromage frais and raisins together and chill overnight before continuing as normal.

Muesli Melons

Serves 2   Total CHO — 50g   Total Cals — 290

---

2 small cantaloup melons
3 heaped tablespoons 8 per cent fat fromage frais
2 tablespoons unsweetened muesli
2 oz (50g) stoned prunes, soaked overnight, then chopped

1. Carefully slice the tops from the melons and scoop out the flesh. Keep the skins whole.
2. Chop the melon flesh and mix with the remaining ingredients.*
3. Return to the skins. Chill for 2 hours and serve.

Each portion contains 25g CHO and 145 calories.

Note: This recipe is *not* suitable for freezing.

* For a sweeter end result, mix the fromage frais and prunes together and leave overnight before continuing as normal.

Oranges in Cointreau

Serves 4   Total CHO — 40g   Total Cals — 160

4 medium oranges
2 tablespoons
Cointreau (orange
liqueur)
¼ pint (150ml)
water

1. Peel the oranges and segment them, removing all the pith and skin.
2. Heat the liqueur and water to boiling point, pour onto the oranges and allow to cool.
3. Chill for 2 hours and serve.

Each portion contains 10g CHO and 40 calories.

Note: This recipe is not suitable for freezing.

Raspberry Parcels

Serves 4   Total CHO — 40g   Total Cals — 180

1 lb (450g) fresh or
frozen raspberries
1 large cooking
apple, peeled, cored
and chopped
4 × 8-inch (20cm)
squares cooking foil

1. Place equal quantities of each fruit in the centre of each foil square.
2. Seal the foil and bake at 300°F/150°C (Gas Mark 2) for 30 minutes. Serve.

Each parcel contains 10g CHO and 45 calories.

Note: This recipe is not suitable for freezing.

Baked Stuffed Pears

Serves 2   Total CHO — 70g   Total Cals — 260

---

2 medium-firm
William pears,
washed and cored
3 oz (75g) mixed
dried fruit
¼ pint (150ml) water

1. Place the pears in an oven-proof dish.
2. Stuff with the dried fruit and pour on the water.
3. Bake at 350°F/180°C (Gas Mark 4) for 15–20 minutes until the pears are tender.

or

Microwave on MEDIUM for 6–8 minutes until the pears are tender.
4. Serve hot or cold.

Each portion contains 35g CHO and 130 calories.

Note: This recipe is not suitable for freezing.

5. Celebration Desserts

Trifle

Serves 6	Total CHO — 95g	Total Cals — 1330

Jelly
15 oz (400g) tin
fruit cocktail in
natural juice
1 sachet gelatine
2 tablespoons
boiling water

Custard
2 tablespoons
custard powder
½ pint (275ml)
skimmed milk

Topping
½ pint (275ml)
whipping cream
Few toasted almonds

1. Drain the fruit (reserving the juice) and place in the base of a serving dish.
2. Make the juice up to ½ pint (285ml) with cold water.
3. Dissolve the gelatine in the boiling water. Stir into the juice and pour over the fruit. Allow to cool until set.
4. Make the custard in usual way, using the skimmed milk. Pour over the jelly. Allow to cool.
5. Top with whipped cream and nuts.

Each portion contains 15g CHO and 220 calories.

Note: This recipe is *not* suitable for freezing.

Traditional Christmas Pudding

Serves 8   Total CHO — 300g   Total Cals — 1570

4 oz (100g) stoned prunes, chopped
3 oz (75g) currants
3 oz (75g) sultanas
2 oz (50g) glâcé cherries, chopped
1 oz (25g) ground almonds
4 oz (100g) wholemeal self-raising flour
2 teaspoons mixed spice
1 medium cooking apple, grated
4 oz (100g) fresh wholemeal breadcrumbs
Juice and rind of 1 lemon
2 size 3 eggs
3 tablespoons semi-skimmed milk
1 tablespoon black treacle

1. Beat all the ingredients together well until the fruit is evenly distributed.
2. Turn into a lightly-oiled 1½ pint (825ml) basin. Cover with greaseproof paper or foil.
3. Steam for 3 hours.

or

Steam for 20 minutes and pressure cook at 15 lb pressure for 1¾ hours.
4. Turn out for 10 minutes before serving.

Each portion contains almost 40g CHO and 195 calories.

Note: This recipe freezes well but if it is not frozen it will only keep for 1 week in the refrigerator. Steaming hints can be found on page 27.

Microwave Christmas Pudding

Serves 8   Total CHO — 245g   Total Cals — 1870

2 oz (50g) fresh
wholemeal
breadcrumbs
3 oz (75g) wholemeal
self-raising flour
Sea salt
Pinch mixed spice
1 oz (25g) glacé
cherries, chopped
3 oz (75g) currants
2 oz (50g) raisins
5 oz (150g) dates,
chopped
2 oz (50g) ground
almonds
1 small cooking
apple, peeled, cored
and chopped
2 oz (50g) chopped
mixed peel
1 large carrot, peeled
and grated
2 teaspoons lemon
juice
3 size 3 eggs
¼ pint (150ml)
skimmed milk
1 tablespoon black
treacle
1 tablespoon brandy

1. Beat all of the ingredients together well.
2. Turn into a lightly-oiled 1½ pint (825ml) basin. Cover with cling-film then pierce the top.
3. Microwave on MEDIUM for 9 minutes, rest for 3 minutes. Microwave again for 9 minutes.
4. Turn out and allow to stand for 5 minutes. Serve.

Each portion contains 30g CHO and 230 calories.

Note: This recipe freezes well, but if not frozen, will only keep for 1 week in the refrigerator.

Reduced-sugar Mincemeat
A healthier alternative

Yields 1 lb 5 oz (600g)
Total CHO — 235g   Total Cals — 1170

12 oz (350g) mixed
dried fruit
4 oz (100g) cooking
apple, peeled and
grated
2 oz (50g) carrot,
grated
2 oz (50g) mixed
nuts, chopped
Juice and grated
rind of 1 large
lemon
1 teaspoon mixed
spice

1. Mix all of the ingredients together well, cover and leave to stand for 24 hours.
2. Blend or liquidize on a high setting for 2 minutes. Pack into sterilized jars and seal with jam pot covers.

or

Place in a plastic box and freeze.

1 oz (25g) of mincemeat contains 10g CHO and 55 calories.

Note: If not frozen, this recipe should only be stored for up to 3 weeks.

Special Christmas Pies

Makes 12   Total CHO — 220g   Total Cals — 2120

Pastry
3 oz (75g)
polyunsaturated
margarine
5 oz (150g)
wholemeal flour
Cold water, as
necessary

Filling
24 teaspoons reduced-
sugar mincemeat
(page 69)
A little brandy

Topping
¼ pint (150ml)
whipping cream

1. Make the pastry by rubbing the fat into flour and bringing to a soft dough with a little water. (A food processor makes good pastry.)

2. Chill for 10 minutes. Using pastry cutters, cut 12 bases and 12 lids.

3. Mix the mincemeat and brandy together. Place the pastry bases in patty tins and fill with 2 teaspoons of the mincemeat mixture.

4. Cut small circles from the centre of the lids and place the lids over the filled bases.

5. Bake at 200°C/400F (Gas Mark 6) for 10–15 minutes. Allow to cool.

6. Whip the cream and spoon into the circles in the lids. Serve.

Each pie contains almost 20g CHO and 175 calories.

Note: This recipe freezes well without the cream.

Frozen Christmas Pud

Serves 5   Total CHO — 130g   Total Cals — 640

---

2 oz (50g) raisins
2 oz (50g) currants
2 oz (50g) glâcé
cherries, chopped
1 tablespoon reduced-
sugar mincemeat
(page 69)
7 fl oz (200ml) carton
semi-skimmed
unsweetened
evaporated milk,
chilled for 2 hours

1. Mix the fruits and the mincemeat together.
2. Whip the milk until thick and moussy.
3. Pour the milk into a large freezer container, cover and freeze until almost solid.
4. Stir in the fruits and freeze again.

Each portion contains 25g CHO and 130 calories.

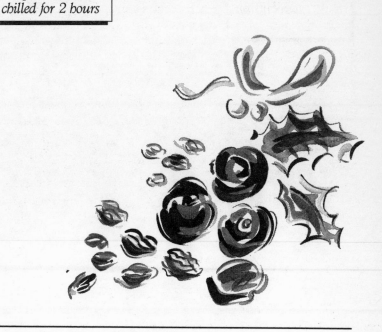

Rum, Fruit and Nut Freeze

Serves 4   Total CHO — 65g   Total Cals — 580

3 oz (75g) fresh
wholemeal
breadcrumbs
1 oz (25g) almonds,
chopped
1 size 3 egg, separated
10 oz (275g) low-fat
natural yogurt
1 oz (25g) dates,
chopped
2 tablespoons rum
or ½ teaspoon rum
essence

1. Mix the breadcrumbs and the nuts together. Place under the grill for 2 minutes or until golden and toasted. Leave to cool.
2. Blend the egg yolk, yogurt, dates and rum. Stir in the nuts and bread.
3. Whisk the egg white until stiff — fold into the mixture carefully.
4. Pour into a freezer container, cover and freeze until firm. Allow to stand in the refrigerator for 30 minutes before serving.

Each portion contains 15g CHO and 145 calories.

Creamy Yogurt Ice-cream

Makes just over ¾ pint (½ litre)
Serves 6   Total CHO — 15g   Total Cals — 690

6 fl oz (180ml) low-
fat natural yogurt
6 fl oz (180ml)
whipping cream

1. Mix the ingredients together well, pour into a freezer container, cover and freeze.
2. When on the point of freezing, whisk or process until thick and the volume has doubled — 2-3 minutes.
3. Return to the freezer, seal well and use as required.

Each portion contains neg CHO and 45 calories.

Coffee Yogurt Ice-cream

Makes just over ¾ pint (½ litre)
Serves 6   Total CHO — 15g   Total Cals — 690

6 fl oz (180ml) low-
fat natural yogurt
6 fl oz (180ml)
whipping cream
1 teaspoon instant
coffee

1. Mix the ingredients together well, pour into a freezer container and freeze.
2. When on the point of freezing, whisk or process until thick and the volume has doubled — 2-3 minutes.
3. Return to the freezer, seal well and use as required.

Each portion contains neg CHO and 45 calories.

Strawberry Ice-cream

Serves 8   Total CHO — 30g   Total Cals — 820

---

1 lb (450g) fresh or
frozen strawberries
1 size 3 egg
2 size 3 egg yolks
¼ pint (150ml) water
5 oz (150g) carton
whipping cream

1. Purée the strawberries and reserve.
2. In a processor or liquidizer beat the egg and yolks together until creamy.
3. Bring the water to the boil and boil for 1 minute.
4. On a high speed, pour the boiling water into the egg mixture and process until thick and moussy (2–3 minutes).
5. Fold the cream into the fruit and gently fold in the egg mousse.
6. Place in a freezer container and freeze.
7. Before serving remove from the freezer for 5 minutes and process for 1 minute. Serve.

Each portion contains neg CHO and 100 calories.

Apricot Ice-cream

Serves 8   Total CHO — 85g   Total Cals — 750

2 × 14oz (400g)
tins apricots in
natural juice
1 size 3 egg
2 size 3 egg yolks
5 oz (150g) 8 per
cent fat fromage
frais

1. Drain the apricots, reserving the juice. Purée the apricots and set aside.
2. Bring ¼ pint (150ml) of the juice to the boil. Boil for 1 minute.
3. In a processor or liquidizer beat the eggs and yolks together until creamy. On a high speed pour on the boiling juice. Process until thick and moussy (2–3 minutes).
4. Fold the fromage frais into the fruit. Gently fold in the egg mousse.
5. Place in a freezer container and freeze.
6. Before serving, remove from the freezer for 5 minutes and process for 1 minute. Serve.

Each portion contains 10g CHO and 95 calories.

Guava Ice-cream

Serves 6   Total CHO — 65g   Total Cals — 650

2 × 10 oz (285g)
tins guavas in
natural juice
1 size 3 egg
1 size 3 egg yolk
5 oz (150g) 8 per
cent fromage frais

1. Drain the guavas, reserving the juice. Purée and sieve to remove the seeds. Set aside.

2. Bring ¼ pint (150ml) of the juice to the boil and boil for 1 minute.

3. In a processor or liquidizer beat the eggs and yolks until creamy. On a high speed pour on the boiling juice. Process until thick and moussy (2-3 minutes).

4. Fold the fromage frais into the fruit. Gently fold in the egg mousse

5. Place in a freezer container and freeze.

6. Before serving, remove from the freezer for 5 minutes and process for 1 minute. Serve.

Each portion contains 10g CHO and 110 calories.

Chocolate Curd Cheese Ice-cream

Serves 4   Total CHO — 20g   Total Cals — 385

4 oz (100g) curd
cheese
4 oz (100g) 8 per
cent fromage frais
5 oz (150g) carton
low-fat yogurt
2 teaspoons drinking
chocolate powder
2 size 3 egg whites

1. Blend the curd cheese, fromage frais, yogurt and chocolate together well.
2. Whisk the egg whites to stiff peaks and gently fold into the mixture.
3. Pour into a freezer container and freeze. Stir gently once during freezing.

Each portion contains 5g CHO and 95 calories.

Coffee Curd Ice-cream

Serves 4   Total CHO — 10g   Total Cals — 350

4 oz (100g) curd
cheese
4 oz (100g) 8 per
cent fat fromage frais
1 teaspoon instant
coffee
1 × 5 oz (150g)
carton low-fat
natural yogurt
2 size 3 egg whites

1. Blend the curd cheese, fromage frais, coffee and yogurt together well.
2. Whisk the egg whites to stiff peaks and gently fold into the mixture.
3. Pour into a freezer container and freeze. Stir gently once during freezing.

Each portion contains neg CHO and 90 calories.

Prune Yogurt Ice-cream

Serves 4   Total CHO — 45g   Total Cals — 810

*6 fl oz (180ml)
whipping cream
6 fl oz (180ml) low-
fat natural yogurt
3 oz (75g) stoned
prunes, puréed*

1. Mix all of the ingredients together well.
2. Pour into a freezer container and freeze. When on the point of freezing, whisk or blend until thick and double in volume.
3. Seal well, freeze and use as required.

Each portion contains 10g CHO and 200 calories.

Fluffy Chiffon Pie

Serves 6   Total CHO — 125g   Total Cals — 1290

Base
4 oz (100g) oats
3 oz (75g) polyunsaturated margarine, melted
1 tablespoon clear honey

Filling
Rind and juice of 1 orange
Rind and juice of 1 lemon
¼ pint (150ml) unsweetened orange juice
1 tablespoon cornflour
2 size 3 eggs, separated

1. Mix all of the base ingredients together and press into the base of a 6-inch (15cm) square cake tin.
2. Blend the rinds and juices with the cornflour and egg yolks and cook over a gentle heat until thick, stirring well. Allow to cool.
3. Whisk the egg whites to stiff peaks. Gently fold into the juice mixture and pour onto the base.
4. Bake at 200°C/400°F (Gas Mark 6) for 15 minutes. Serve immediately.

Each portion contains 20g CHO and 215 calories.

Note: This recipe is not suitable for freezing.

Strawberry Choux Circle

Serves 6   Total CHO — 90g   Total Cals — 1140

Choux Pastry
¼ pint (150ml) water
2 oz (50g)
polyunsaturated
margarine
3 oz (75g)
wholemeal flour
2 size 3 eggs

Filling
1½ lb (675g)
strawberries, fresh or
frozen, chopped
8 oz (225g) natural
cottage cheese

1. Heat the water and margarine in a heavy-based pan until the margarine has melted. Quickly beat in the flour to a stiff dough.
2. Remove the pan from the heat, add the eggs one at a time, beat well until the mixture leaves the sides of the pan and is glossy.
3. Spoon mixture around a non-stick 8-inch (20cm) flan tin and bake at 220°C/425°F (Gas Mark 7) for 15-20 minutes.
4. Allow to cool on a wire rack.
5. Mix the fruit and cheese together and pile into the ring. Serve.

Each portion contains 15g CHO and 190 calories.

Note: This recipe is *not* suitable for freezing.

Wholemeal Rough Puff Pastry

Makes 8 oz (225g)
Total CHO — 115g   Total Cals — 1100

6 oz (175g)
wholemeal flour
Sea salt
3 oz (75g)
polyunsaturated
margarine
Cold water, as
necessary

1. Mix the flour and salt in a large bowl.
2. Chop the fat into walnut-size pieces and gently stir into the flour.
3. Use the cold water to bring the dough together (the fat will still be in lumps).
4. Turn out onto a lightly-floured board and roll to a rectangle.
5. Fold the rectangle into 3 by bringing the top third down and the bottom third up. Turn through 90° and roll again. Repeat twice.
6. Chill the pastry for 20 minutes and use as required.

Note: This pastry freezes well *raw*.

Peach and Cottage Cheese Bouche

Makes 5   Total CHO — 145g   Total Cals — 1365

*8 oz/225g quantity
Rough Puff Pastry
(page 79)
3 fresh peaches or
6 peach halves tinned
in juice, drained
5 oz (150g) cottage
cheese, sieved*

1. Roll pastry to ¼-inch (0.5cm) thick, cut out five 4-inch (10cm) circles and place on a baking sheet. Cut an inner circle 1-inch (2.5cm) inside each bouche, only cutting two-thirds of the way into the pastry.

2. Bake at 400°F/200°C (Gas Mark 6) for 15–20 minutes until risen and golden brown. Allow to cool on a wire rack. Scoop out centre rings, leaving the cases intact, and reserve.

3. Mix the chopped fruit and cottage cheese together and pile into the cases. Return the pastry tops and serve.

Each portion contains 30g CHO and 270 calories.

Note: This recipe is *not* suitable for freezing.

Summary Fruit Vol-au-vents

Makes 8   Total CHO — 130g   Total Cals — 1170

8 oz (225g) quantity Rough Puff Pastry (page 79)
6 oz (175g) fresh strawberries, chopped
4 oz (100g) fresh raspberries, chopped

1. Roll the pastry to ¼-inch (0.5cm) thick and cut out 8 small vol-au-vent cases. Place on a baking sheet. Cut an inner circle about ½-inch (1cm) inside only cutting two-thirds of the way into the pastry.

2. Bake at 400°F/200°C (Gas Mark 6) for 10–15 minutes. Allow to cool on a wire rack. Scoop out centres, leaving the cases intact, and reserve.

3. Mix the chopped fruits and pile into the cases. Return the tops and serve.

Each vol-au-vent contains almost 15g CHO and 145 calories.

Note: This recipe is *not* suitable for freezing.

Mandarin Vol-au-vents

Makes 10   Total CHO — 145g   Total Cals — 1700

8 oz (225g) quantity
Rough Puff Pastry
(page 79)
5 oz (150g) carton
whipping cream
½ × 10 oz (275g)
tin mandarins in
natural juice,
drained

1. Roll the pastry to ¼-inch (0.5cm) thick and cut out 10 small vol-au-vent cases. Place on a baking sheet. Cut an inner circle ½-inch (1cm) inside each case, only cutting two-thirds of the way through the pastry.
2. Bake at 400°F/200°C (Gas Mark 6) for 10–15 minutes. Allow to cool on a wire rack. Scoop out the centres, leaving the cases intact, and reserve.
3. Whip the cream to soft peaks and mix in the chopped fruit. Pile into cases, return the tops and serve.

Each vol-au-vent contains 15g CHO and 170 calories.

Note: This recipe is not suitable for freezing.

Millefeuille

Serves 10   Total CHO — 150g   Total Cals — 1750

---

8 oz (225g) quantity
Rough Puff Pastry
(page 79)
5 oz (150g) carton
whipping cream
3 tablespoons
reduced-sugar jam

1. Roll the pastry to an ⅛-inch (3mm) thick oblong and cut into 3 equal rectangles. Place on baking sheets.
2. Bake at 400°F/200°C (Gas Mark 6) for 10–15 minutes. Allow to cool on a wire rack.
3. Whip cream to soft peaks. Spread half the jam on top of one of the pastry layers and top with one third of the cream. Repeat with two more layers ending with the cream. Serve immediately.

Each portion contains 15g CHO and 175 calories.

Note: This recipe is *not* suitable for freezing.

Mandarin Cheesecake

Serves 6   Total CHO — 165g   Total Cals — 1850

Base
7 oz (200g) digestive
biscuits
3 oz (75g)
polyunsaturated
margarine

Topping
1 × 10 oz (275g) tin
mandarins in
natural juice,
drained
1 sachet gelatine
2 tablespoons boiling
water
5 oz (150g) cottage
cheese
5 oz (150g) carton
low-fat natural
yogurt

1. Crush the biscuits and melt the margarine — mix them together well and press into the base of a 8-inch (20cm) flan dish. Chill for 20 minutes.
2. Place the mandarins in a mixing bowl and crush with the back of a wooden spoon.
3. Dissolve the gelatine in the boiling water. Stir the cheese and yogurt into the oranges. Beat in the gelatine. Pour over the base.;
4. Refrigerate until set.

Each portion contains 30g CHO and 310 calories.

Note: This recipe is not suitable for freezing.

Pineapple Cheesecake

Serves 5   Total CHO — 140   Total Cals — 1400

Base
4 oz (100g) rolled oats
3 oz (75g)
polyunsaturated
margarine, melted
1 tablespoon clear
honey

Topping
5 oz (150g) 1 per
cent fromage frais
5 oz (150g) cottage
cheese
15 oz (400g) tin
crushed pineapple in
natural juice,
drained

1. Mix all the base ingredients together well and press into the base of a 8-inch (20cm) flan ring. Bake at 350°F/180°C (Gas Mark 4) for 15 minutes. Allow to cool.
2. Blend all the topping ingredients together well and pour over the base. Chill and serve.

Each portion contains almost 30g CHO and 280 calories.

Note: This recipe is *not* suitable for freezing.

Pineapple Gâteau

Slices into 8   Total CHO — 185g   Total Cals — 1825

1 medium cooking
apple, peeled, cored
and chopped
1 oz (25g) dried figs,
chopped
1 oz (25g) raisins,
chopped
3 oz (75g)
polyunsaturated
margarine
2 size 3 eggs
6 oz (175g)
wholemeal self-
raising flour
A little skimmed
milk
½ quantity
Pineapple Cream
(page 94)

1. Cream the apple, figs, raisins and margarine together well until light, fluffy and smooth — a processor is the easiest way.

2. Beat in the eggs, fold in the flour and enough milk to bring to a soft dough.

3. Pour into a lightly-oiled loose-bottom 8-inch (20cm) cake tin.

4. Bake at 180°C/350°F (Gas Mark 4) for 30 minutes or until firm to the touch. Remove from the tin and allow to cool on a wire rack.

5. Slice through horizontally. Sandwich together and top with the Pineapple Cream.

Each portion contains almost 25g CHO and 230 calories.

Note: The sponge freezes well empty.

Strawberry Cheese Gâteau

Slices into 8   Total CHO — 175g   Total Cals — 1570

1 medium cooking
apple, peeled, cored
and chopped
1 oz (25g) dried figs,
chopped
1 oz (25g) raisins,
chopped
3 oz (75g)
polyunsaturated
margarine
2 size 3 eggs
6 oz (175g)
wholemeal self-
raising flour
A little skimmed
milk
8 oz (225g)
strawberries, fresh or
frozen, chopped
8 oz (225g) 1 per
cent fromage frais

1. Cream the apple, figs, raisins and margarine well until light, fluffy and smooth — a food processor is the easiest way.

2. Beat in the eggs, fold in the flour and enough milk to bring to a soft dough.

3. Pour into a lightly-oiled loose-bottom 8-inch (20cm) cake tin.

4. Bake at 180°C/350°F (Gas Mark 4) for 30 minutes or until firm to the touch. Remove from the tin and allow to cool on a wire rack.

5. Slice through horizontally.

6. Beat together the strawberries and fromage frais — use to sandwich the sponge together and as a topping.

Each portion contains 20g CHO and 195 calories.

Note: The sponge freezes well *empty*.

Carob Nut Gâteau

Slices into 8   Total CHO — 155g   Total Cals — 1920

1 medium cooking apple, peeled, cored and chopped
1 oz (25g) dried figs, chopped
1 oz (25g) raisins, chopped
3 oz (75g) polyunsaturated margarine
2 size 3 eggs
5 oz (150g) self-raising flour
1 oz (25g) carob powder
A little skimmed milk
5 oz (150g) carton whipping cream
2 oz (50g) chopped nuts

1. Cream the apple, figs, raisins and margarine together well until light, fluffy and smooth — a food processor is the easiest way.
2. Beat in the eggs, mix together the flour and carob powder and fold into the eggs with enough milk to bring to a soft dough.
3. Pour into a lightly-oiled loose-bottom 8-inch (20cm) cake tin.
4. Bake at 180°C/350°F (Gas Mark 4) for 30 minutes or until firm to the touch. Remove from tin and allow to cool on a wire rack.
5. Slice through horizontally.
6. Whip the cream to soft peaks and use to sandwich the layers and as a topping. Sprinkle with the nuts.

Each portion contains 20g CHO and 240 calories.

Note: The sponge freezes well empty.

Apricot Gâteau

Slices into 8   Total CHO — 125g   Total Cals — 965

3 size 3 eggs
1½ oz (37g) sugar *
4 oz (100g)
wholemeal self-
raising flour
2 oz (50g) dried
apricots, soaked and
chopped
8 oz (225g) cottage
cheese, sieved

1. Whisk the eggs and sugar together until thick and foamy (a food processor is *not* successful).

2. Gently fold in the flour and pour into two loose-bottomed, lightly-oiled 8-inch (20cm) cake tins.

3. Bake at 180°C/350°F (Gas Mark 4) for 15 minutes until springy to the touch. Allow to cool on a wire rack.

4. Beat together the apricots and sieved cheese. Use to sandwich the layers together and as a topping.

Each portion contains 15g CHO and 120 calories.

Note: This sponge freezes well *empty*.

* Between 8 people this amount of sugar becomes irrelevant.

Chocolate Mint Gâteau

Slices into 6   Total CHO — 100g   Total Cals — 1345

3 size 3 eggs
1½ oz (37g) sugar*
3 oz (75g)
wholemeal self-
raising flour
1 oz (25g) carob
powder
5 oz (150g) carton
whipping cream
Peppermint essence
2 oz (50g) chopped
nuts

1. Whisk the eggs and sugar together until thick and foamy (a processor is *not* successful).

2. Mix the flour and carob powder together. Gently fold into the egg mixture and pour into 2 loose-bottom, lightly-oiled 8-inch (20cm) cake tins.

3. Bake at 180°C/350°F (Gas Mark 4) for 15 minutes until springy to the touch. Allow to cool on a wire rack.

4. Whip the cream to soft peaks, flavour with the essence and stir in the nuts.

5. Use to sandwich the sponge together and as a topping.

Each portion contains about 15g CHO and 225 calories.

Note: This sponge freezes well *empty*.

* Between 6 people this amount of sugar becomes irrelevant.

Black Forest Gâteau

Slices into 8   Total CHO — 120g   Total Cals — 1240

3 size 3 eggs
1½ oz (37g) sugar*
3 oz (75g)
wholemeal self-
raising flour
1 oz (25g) carob
powder
6 oz (175g) black
cherries, fresh or
tinned in natural
juice, stoned
5 oz (150g) carton
whipping cream

1. Whisk the eggs and sugar together until thick and foamy (a processor is *not* successful).

2. Mix the flour and carob powder together. Gently fold into the egg mixture and pour into 2 loose-bottom, lightly-oiled 8-inch (20cm) cake tins.

3. Bake at 180°C/350°F (Gas Mark 4) for 15 minutes until springy to the touch. Allow to cool on a wire rack.

4. Chop the cherries. Whisk the cream to soft peaks and fold into the fruit. Use to sandwich the sponge together and as a topping.

Each portion contains 15g CHO and 155 calories.

Note: The sponge freezes well *empty*.

* Between 8 people this amount of sugar becomes irrelevant.

Blackberry Mousse

Serves 6   Total CHO — 30g   Total Cals — 330

---

*10 oz (275g) tin
blackberries in
natural juice
8 oz (225g) Quark
cheese
2 egg whites,
whisked to stiff
peaks*

1. Blend the fruit and cheese together until smooth.
2. Gently fold in the egg whites. Pour into a serving dish and chill for 2 hours.

Each portion contains 5g CHO and 55 calories.

Note: This recipe is *not* suitable for freezing.

Apricot and Orange Mousse

Makes 4 large portions
Total CHO — 80g   Total Cals — 520

14 oz (400g) tin
apricots in natural
juice
1 tablespoon reduced-
sugar orange
marmalade
1 sachet gelatine
2 tablespoons
boiling water
7 fl oz (200ml)
carton semi-
skimmed,
unsweetened
evaporated
milk, chilled for 2
hours

1. Purée the apricots and the marmalade together.
2. Dissolve the gelatine in the water and stir into the purée.
3. Whip the milk until thick and glossy. Gently fold into the fruit mixture. Chill until set.

Each portion contains 20g CHO and 130 calories.

Note: This recipe is not suitable for freezing.

Pineapple Cream

Serves 6   Total CHO — 60g   Total Cals — 835

---

*14 oz (400g) tin
crushed pineapple in
natural juice
8 oz (225g) 1 per
cent fromage frais
1 sachet gelatine
2 tablespoons
boiling water
5 oz (150g) carton
whipping cream*

1. Mix the pineapple and fromage frais together. Dissolve the gelatine in the water and stir into the pineapple mixture.

2. Whip the cream to stiff peaks and fold into the pineapple mixture.

3. Pour into a serving dish and chill until set.

Each portion contains 10g CHO and 140 calories.

Note: This recipe is *not* suitable for freezing.

Rhubarb Fool

Serves 6   Total CHO — 10g   Total Cals — 545

---

1 lb (450g) rhubarb,
cleaned
5 oz (150g) carton
whipping cream
2 size 3 egg whites

1. Chop the rhubarb and stew in a very little water until tender. Mash or purée and allow to cool.

2. Whip the cream to soft peaks and whisk the egg whites until stiff. Fold together gently.

3. Fold the fruit into the cream and chill before serving.

Each portion contains neg CHO and 90 calories.

Note: This recipe is *not* suitable for freezing.

Chocolate Mousse

Serves 6 　　　Total CHO — 60g 　　　Total Cals — 900

2 × 5 oz (150g)
bars fructose-
sweetened diabetic
chocolate
3 tablespoons
unsweetened orange
juice
3 size 3 eggs,
separated

1. Gently melt the chocolate with the orange juice in a bowl over a pan of hot water.
2. Allow to cool slightly and beat in the egg yolks.
3. Whisk the egg whites to stiff peaks and gently fold into the chocolate mixture. Chill before serving.

Each portion contains 10g CHO and 150 calories.

Note: This recipe is *not* suitable for freezing.

6. Menu Suggestions

Here are some ideas for desserts to fit into your menus. These should obviously be used with high-fibre, low-fat first courses, and fit into your carbohydrate and calorie allowances.

MENU 1
A Summer Wedding Buffet

Strawberry Shortcake (page 45)
Apricot Trifle (page 53)
Peach and Cottage Cheese Bouche (page 80)
Pineapple Gâteau (page 86)
Blackberry Mousse (page 92)

MENU 2
A Winter Sunday Lunch Party

Plums in a Veil (page 20)
Sultana and Gooseberry Pudding (page 23)
Pear and Almond Flan (page 28)
Boozy Orange Crêpes (page 31)
Hot Fruit Salad (page 41)

MENU 3
A 'Freeze Ahead' Selection

Apple and Raisin Tart (page 35)
Rum, Fruit and Nut Freeze (page 70)

Frozen Christmas Pud (page 69)
Orange and Apple Brown Betty (page 17)
Apricot Upside-down Pudding (page 19)

MENU 4
Packed Lunch Suggestions

One portion Creamy Orange Whip (page 37)
Caribbean Flan (page 26)
Pear and Mincemeat Flan (page 27)
Plum and Almond Pie (page 36)

MENU 5
Low-calorie Puddings

Creamy Orange Whip (page 37)
Blackcurrant Whip (page 38)
Apple Snow (page 39)
Jelly Castles (page 40)
Hot Fruit Salad (page 41)

MENU 6
Special Occasions Only!!

Chocolate Mousse (page 96)
Millefeuille (page 83)
Black Forest Gâteau (page 91)
Carob Nut Gâteau (page 88)

MENU 7
Puddings in a Hurry

Hot Fruit Salad (page 41)
Two-colour Fruit Salad (page 40)
Cheesy Peaches (page 42)
Rum, Raisin and Apricot Yogurt (page 54)
Muesli Cottage Cheese (page 56)

Recommended Reading

These books contain lots of helpful information and many recipes which you can use for diabetic desserts.

Countdown
(Published by the British Diabetic Association)
A guide to the carbohydrate and calorie content of manufactured foods.

Christmas Cookery
(Published by the British Diabetic Association)
A recipe leaflet by Sue Hall.

Packed Lunches and Snacks
(Published by Thorsons Publishing Group, 1986)
A recipe book by Sue Hall.

Simple Home Baking
(Published by the British Diabetic Association)
A recipe leaflet by Sue Hall.

Diabetic Cooking for One
(Published by Thorsons Publishing Group, 1987)
A recipe book by Sue Hall.

The Diabetic's Microwave Cookbook
(Published by Thorsons Publishing Group, 1986)
A microwave book by Sue Hall.

The Diabetes Handbook — Non-Insulin Dependent Diabetes
(Published by Thorsons Publishing Group, 1986)
By Dr John Day.

The Diabetes Handbook — Insulin Dependent Diabetes
(Published by Thorsons Publishing Group, 1986)
By Dr John Day.

Sugar-Free Cakes and Biscuits
(Published by Faber and Faber, 1985)
A recipe book by Elbie Lebrecht.

Cooking for Your Diabetic Child
(Published by Thorsons Publishing Group, 1988)
A recipe book by Sue Hall.

Appendix:
List of Food Values

Food	Portion	gCHO	Cals
Almonds — chopped	1 oz (25g)	2	110
— ground	1 oz (25g)	1	160
Apple — eating, raw	1	10	40
— cooking, raw	1 lb (450g)	35	140
— juice, unsweetened	½ pint (275ml)	35	130
Apricots — dried	1 oz (25g)	12	50
— fresh	1 lb (450g)	30	125
— tinned in natural juice	1×14 oz (400g) tin	40	190
Banana — raw	1 medium	10	40
Biscuits — digestive	1	10	70
Blackberries — raw	1 lb (450g)	30	130
Bread — wholemeal	1 oz (25g)	10	60
Carob powder	2 tablespoons	10	50
Carrot — raw	1 lb (450g)	20	100
Cherries — glacé	1 oz (25g)	15	55
Cherries — black canned in natural juice	1×14 oz (400g) tin	40	190
Cheese — cottage	1 oz (25g)	neg	27
— curd	1 oz (25g)	neg	40
— Quark	1 oz (25g)	2	25
— Ricotta	1 oz (25g)	neg	40
Chocolate — diabetic	1 oz (25g)	10	115
Cider — dry	½ pint (275ml)	4	110
Clementines — raw	1	5	20

Food	Portion	gCHO	Cals
Coconut — desiccated	1 oz (25g)	1	170
Cornflour	1 oz (25g)	26	100
Cream — whipping	1 oz (25g)	½	80
Currants — dried	1 oz (25g)	18	70
Custard powder	1 oz (25g)	26	100
Dates — dried	1 oz (25g)	18	70
Drinking chocolate	1 teaspoon	5	20
Egg — size 3	1	—	74
Figs — dried	1 oz (25g)	13	55
Flour — wholemeal plain and self-raising	1 oz (25g)	18	90
— 81 per cent plain and self-raising	1 oz (25g)	19	92
Fromage frais — 1 per cent fat	1 oz (25g)	neg	15
Fromage frais — 8 per cent fat	1 oz (25g)	neg	25
Fruit salad — dried	1 oz (25g)	10	40
Fruit cocktail — tinned in natural juice	1×14 oz (400g) tin	50	190
Fructose	1 oz (25g)	30*	115
Gelatine	1 sachet	—	35
Gooseberries — fresh	1 lb (450g)	15	80
Grapes	1 lb (450g)	65	225
Hazelnuts	1 oz (25g)	2	110
Honey	1 oz (25g)	20	80
Jam — reduced-sugar	1 oz (25g)	10	30
Mandarins — tinned in natural juice	1×10 oz (275g) tin	25	100
Margarine — polyunsaturated	1 oz (25g)	—	210
Marmalade — reduced-sugar	1 oz (25g)	10	30

* Usually ignored if less than 1 oz (25g) eaten per day.

Food	Portion	gCHO	Cals
Melon — fresh	1 lb (450g)	13	60
Milk — fresh skimmed	1 pint (550ml)	30	190
— fresh semi-skimmed	1 pint (550ml)	30	260
— evaporated skimmed	4 oz (100g)	13	120
— evaporated whole	1×14 oz (400g) tin	40	650
Mincemeat — reduced-sugar	1 oz (25g)	10	30
Muesli — unsweetened	1 oz (25g)	18	100
Nuts — mixed	1 oz (25g)	2	110
Oats — rolled	1 oz (25g)	20	110
Oranges — fresh, whole	1	10	40
— juice, unsweetened	½ pint (275ml)	30	120
Peaches — fresh	1	10	40
— tinned in natural juice	1×14 oz (400g) tin	45	180
Peel — chopped mixed	1 oz (25g)	18	70
Pears — fresh	1	10	40
— tinned in natural juice	1×14 oz (400g) tin	40	160
Pineapple — tinned in natural juice	1×14 oz (400g) tin	55	240
Plums — raw	1 lb (450g)	40	160
Raisins	1 oz (25g)	18	70
Raspberries — raw	1 lb (450g)	25	110
Rhubarb — raw	1 lb (450g)	5	30
Rice — brown pudding	1 oz (25g)	21	105
Sponge — wholemeal	1 oz (25g)	10	100
Strawberries — raw	1 lb (450g)	27	110
Sugar	1 oz (25g)	25	100
Sultanas	1 oz (25g)	18	70
Treacle — black	1 oz (25g)	10	40
Weetabix	1 biscuit	12	60
Wheatflakes	1 oz (25g)	22	100

Food	Portion	gCHO	Cals
Yogurt — natural low-fat	1×5 oz (150g) carton	10	80
— diet fruit	1×5 oz (150g) carton	7	55

Further Information

BRITISH DIABETIC ASSOCIATION

Diabetes affects just over two per cent of the UK population. Although it cannot be cured or prevented, it can be controlled by proper treatment. However, there may be times when you need further advice and this is where the *British Diabetic Association* (BDA) can help.

The BDA is an independent registered charity with over 105,000 members and 350 local branches. It represents all diabetics and has become increasingly influential in matters concerning the individual.

The Association provides information and practical advice for diabetics and their families. A wide range of literature, goods and videos are available on all aspects of diabetes including *Countdown*, a useful guide to the calorie and carbohydrate values of over 5000 manufactured foods.

The BDA's magazine *Balance* is published every two months and is sent free to members or is available from newsagents, price 85p. It keeps readers up-to-date with the latest medical news, local events, and includes articles on living with diabetes. All diabetics have to follow a lifelong diet and *Balance* gives recipes and dietary information to help bring interest and variety to eating.

Educational and activity holidays are organized for diabetics of every age group, plus teach-in weekends for families with diabetic children or teenagers.

The Association also supports research to find ways to improve treatment and to prevent or cure diabetes. Currently budgeting over

£1.5 million each year, the BDA is the largest single contributor to diabetic research in the UK.

For over 50 years, the BDA has strived to achieve its aims. But it has only been able to do so with the help of its members and supporters. Please join the BDA by completing the application form and sending it with your subscription to:

British Diabetic Association
10 Queen Anne Street
London W1M 0BD

Tel: 01-323 1531

Enrolment Form

The British Diabetic Association
10 Queen Anne Street
London W1M 0BD

MEMBERSHIP SUBSCRIPTIONS

Life membership	Single payment of £105 or £15 a year for 7 years
Annual membership	£5 a year
Reduced Rate Membership (pensioners, students on Government grant and those in receipt of DHSS benefits)	£1 a year
Overseas annual membership	£10 a year
Overseas life membership	Single payment of £150

Please enrol me as a:

☐ Life Member: £105 or £15 a year for 7 years

☐ Annual Member: £5

☐ Reduced Rate Member: £1

☐ Overseas Life Member: £150

☐ Overseas Annual Member: £10

☐ Are you joining on behalf of a child?
(Children in the UK under the age of 16 can join free for one year if they wish)

I enclose Remittance/Banker's Order for £ ....
(Please delete whichever does not apply)

Date................................Signature....................................

Full name: Mr/Mrs/Miss..
(Block Capitals please)

Address ....

....

Date of Birth.............................Occupation..............................
(This information will be treated as strictly confidential)

Index